OUR ROYAL HERITAGE
Godfrey Talbot

The illustrations and the text of this book distil the essence of the British Monarchy during the Queen's lifetime. Here are pictures of the great ceremonial occasions: the Coronation, Trooping the Colour, the Opening of Parliament, visits of foreign Heads of State, banquets at the Guildhall, and the rest; here are Buckingham Palace, Windsor Castle, Holyroodhouse, and the other royal homes; here is the Queen when she was still Princess Elizabeth, with her royal father, and in the Auxiliary Territorial Service. And here are the other members of the Royal Family who play so great a part both in the Queen's life and in that of the nation, chief among them, of course, the Queen Mother, Prince Philip and the Prince of Wales. In addition to the more formal pictures, the informal side of royalty is represented by scenes, for example, at the races, riding and sailing at Cowes.

It would be a mistake, in what is primarily a picture book, to under-estimate the importance of the text. Godfrey Talbot has had more experience as a royal commentator than anyone else alive. He knows how conscientious and hard-working the Queen and her family are and he knows too what a vital role the monarchy has played in giving a sense of national continuity and permanence at a time of unprecedented change. That is the message which he, and the illustrations, very convincingly convey.

48 pages
18 colour plates
12 black and white pictures

(Overleaf)
The Queen at the Royal Maundy ceremony with the Archbishop of Canterbury

OUR ROYAL HERITAGE

Godfrey Talbot,

M.V.O., O.B.E.

B. T. Batsford Ltd. London

Acknowledgements

The author and publishers would like to thank the following for their permission to reproduce the illustrations in this book: British Tourist Authority, pages 36, 37; Camera Press Ltd, pages 13, 31, 46, 47; Central Press Photos Ltd, pages 2, 17, 23, 40, 42, 44; Central Office of Information, pages 38, 45; Fox Photos Ltd, pages 6, 15, 18, 20, 25, 29, 41, 43, 48; the late Noel Habgood, page 34; Paul Popper Ltd, pages 8, 11, 39; the Press Association, pages 26, 32; Kenneth Scowen, FIIP, FRPS, page 35.

First published 1977
Copyright Godfrey Talbot 1977

Made and Printed in Great Britain
by Cox & Wyman Ltd
Fakenham, Norfolk
for the Publishers, B. T. Batsford Ltd
4 Fitzhardinge Street, London W1H 0AH

ISBN 0 7134 0447 7

Contents

(Overleaf)
The Queen addresses the Trades Union
Congress at a Guildhall banquet on the
occasion of their Centenary

Introduction

In an era of universal political and social upheaval, turbulent years of toppled Thrones, an iconoclastic age in which most nations of the world are Republics and most Heads of State are Presidents, the British Monarchy and its Queen remain wanted and are eminently enduring. Crown and wearer stand together in high regard.

When we think of the Monarchy we think of people, the Royal Family, a particularly well known group of distinctive persons, no longer adulated from afar as a collection of almost fairytale puppets as royalty was in the past, but clinically weighed and watched with interest as human beings who play leading parts in the overt national life. Much of their work consists of being photogenically engaged upon public duties and ceremonies on our behalf. Their lawful occasions, and now their personal pursuits too, are daily in the news. Their job is representation, and they are custodians of the traditions and pageants of the seasons.

At the head of this First Family is Queen Elizabeth the Second, Britain's Number One Public Servant, prime focus of loyalty and ideals. Her Majesty reigns but does not rule, yet, as the Sovereign, she is the country's constitutional linch-pin, symbol of law and authority. More than that, she is today a personal repository of unique knowledge of the world and its peoples and affairs. A wide variety of countries acknowledge her as their Head. At first-hand she knows them, and they know her. In her office resides the essence of nation and Commonwealth and in her character a treasury of wisdom and experience.

Ever since she came to the Throne – and a quarter of a century has passed since then – Her Majesty, whilst assiduous in keeping up popular and meaningful customs and historic procedure, has gradually established new patterns of official and personal informality. By travelling on duty a great deal, by the judicious use of film and television and radio, and at the same time by patently enjoying her own serene family life as a modern wife and mother, she has moved with the times and nearer to her subjects. The Monarchy has become adaptable under her hand, so that no longer can it be said that the Palace is one world and the people quite another.

We have an observed and observant Queen, no Pasteboard Britannia.

In the 25 years leading to the Silver Jubilee of the reign, during which the world has undergone so much change and decay, the Royal House has come to stand as something steadfast and dependable, a bulwark against extremism. For under this Queen our Monarchy may be seen as a rock of polished sensibleness and decency in the shifting sands of politics and the scummy tides of fashionable denigration. It is a model of hard,

albeit picturesque work; and its chief worker, a personable woman now in the middle years of her life, has become a Head of State who is wise and well able to exercise the constitutional monarch's constitutional right which has never been better stated than in Walter Bagehot's expression over a hundred years ago: 'To be consulted, to encourage, and to warn.'

We can be proud of the chronicle of the reign. Pleasure in the pageantry of it is natural and salutary. There is nothing to be ashamed of in liking to watch beautifully executed State events or to turn the album photographs of them. The illustrations in this book are evidence that both the high ceremonial and the homely scenes are attractive. Many pictures are of the full-dress occasions which form an outward manifestation of the Queen's work; and these grand happenings are also important in themselves. Part of the Sovereign's function is to maintain dignity. And, dear me, we can do with it! For taste and style are increasingly precious nowadays to leaven slipshod and mannerless times whose stamp is not the graceful bow but the wolf whistle.

The Royal Family is not of course a *typical* family, not characteristic of all of us and certainly not classless. There is no need to imagine that it is any such thing, or want it to be so. It is precisely *not* the business of the Queen and her relatives to go about pretending that they are Mr and Mrs Ordinary Citizen. A Head of State without stardom and a First Family without separateness would make a nonsense of symbolic and constitutional royalty. The life and work of the Family is looked to by millions of people as something distinct and elevated which must shine and glow, with a touch of the old aura of majesty and mystery still about it. Remote in a way, yet close at hand they are, for the Family are *ours,* part of our land and part of our history. The story of the Second Elizabeth is the story of our times.

When she was born – a Londoner, in a Mayfair house on 21 April, 1926 – it was into a world very different from today's. By comparison it was still almost Victorian, assured and respectable and static (that springtime's General Strike notwithstanding). Old King George the Fifth ruled paternally over a great Empire, and flag-waving loyalty to crown and country was the accepted norm at home and overseas.

Not that anybody could foresee the little Princess Elizabeth ever wearing the Crown. She was simply the daughter of the Monarch's second son, the Duke of York. It was her Uncle David, the popular Prince of Wales, golden boy of the 20s, who would one day succeed to the Throne and in due course it would be *his* line who would be the future rulers. And come to the Throne that eldest son duly did, when George the Fifth died

Princess Elizabeth learning how to change
a wheel at an A.T.S. training centre

early in 1936. He came as King Edward the Eighth, bright centre of hopes that were not
to be fulfilled. For, sensationally abdicating to marry the American divorcée he loved, he
reigned for less than a year. Suddenly, against all expectations, his niece's father was
King and she the Heir – at ten years old. Her home now was Buckingham Palace, the
British Sovereign's mansion in the middle of London, a palace which was now housing
its third reigning king within the space of 12 months. An unsettling time.

But the new King, George the Sixth, shy and far from robust though he was, wearer
of an utterly unsought and unprepared-for Crown, lived and reigned for 15 years,
gained the admiration of the British people he led through all the suffering of the Second
World War, and restored the prestige of the Monarchy. He was a man of courage and
discipline, exemplary family life and a strong sense of duty. Immeasurably helped by his
wonderful partner and Queen – today's Queen Elizabeth the Queen Mother – he set
about the task of bringing up not only a daughter but a future Sovereign. Without doubt
the present Queen's application and her grasp of public affairs owes much to the
foundation laid in those early years when a diligent father allowed the Princess to include
in her education a knowledge, from standing beside him, of the stream of dispatches and
State papers which flowed across his desk day in and day out.

Her training and the beginnings of introduction to her destiny progressed even in
wartime. With her sister Margaret, nearly four years younger, the Princess lived quietly
at Windsor Castle during much of the Hitler Years. For the two princesses it was a time
of private education, out of the limelight; but Elizabeth was anxious to share as much
as possible in the activities of her age and generation on the Home Front. In 1942, as
soon as she reached her sixteenth birthday, she presented herself at a Labour Exchange
(wearing her Girl Guide uniform) and registered for National Service. Later, when she
was old enough for that, she got into khaki – and into overalls, becoming qualified, as a
junior officer in a transport section of the Auxiliary Territorial Service, 'to drive and
maintain all classes of military vehicles.'

The Queen is a driver still, but of her own car rather than army trucks, and that
rarely. Her transport is more often a chauffeur-driven royal limousine or an open,
horse-drawn landau in which she moves as Head of State on public view along the
bedecked roads of ceremonial London or, in due season, on the buoyant turf of Royal
Ascot. As to private riding, the sort she most enjoys is horseback. Her Majesty has been
a lover of animals, of horses and dogs and the outdoor occupations of a countrywoman,
from childhood; and those who know will tell you that the quality of her horse-riding

for sheer pleasure in the wide spaces of Windsor or Balmoral Castle matches the schooled excellence of her uniformed, side-saddle appearances before the crowds as she reviews her Household Cavalry and regiments of Foot Guards at the annual spectacle of Trooping the Colour at the beginning of June in London.

She has not overmuch time for relaxation these days. Looking back, it was in the years just after the war that Princess Elizabeth was able for a while to enjoy some real private life and tranquillity, and personal happiness unalloyed by either family worry or responsibility of high office. And she was then in love. Her marriage to Lieutenant Philip Mountbatten, R.N. – a breezily English sailor, though in fact Corfu-born, the son of Prince Andrew and Princess Alice of Greece – was the highlight of 1947, shining briefly but brilliantly through the austerity and gloomy restrictions of that difficult time. Prince Philip – who is still generally and not incorrectly called that – was created Duke of Edinburgh on the eve of the wedding (in fact there wasn't time to alter the marriage-service printing, and the wedding order we had in our hands in Westminster Abbey on 20 November still said that the King's daughter was marrying a naval two-ringer, not a royal peer).

The Princess had celebrated her twenty-first birthday a few months earlier during a tour of South Africa with her parents, and in a world broadcast from Cape Town had dedicated her 'whole life, whether it be long or short', to the service of the Commonwealth – a pledge unswervingly implemented to this day.

But soon after the marriage there came, and came to stay across her life, a cloud of nagging anxiety over her father's frail and failing health. When Her Royal Highness and her husband undertook overseas tours on the King's behalf, she had to carry with her an Accession to the Throne declaration – her own accession – in a sealed envelope to be opened if the King died. And she and Prince Philip were indeed abroad on duty, in Kenya at the start of what was to have been a long journey to Australia and New Zealand, when George the Sixth died in his sleep 4,000 miles away at Sandringham House in Norfolk, the place where he had been born 56 years before.

He died on 6 February, 1952. And Elizabeth was Queen Regnant at the age of 25.

Her reign began at once, but it was not until a full 16 months after daughter had succeeded father that there took place the resplendent rite of the Coronation. This was the pageant of the century, impressive in its solemnity, magnificent in ancient ecclesiastical ritual, exhilarating in the long street processions in spite of the June rain – and everything superbly stage-managed by the expert Duke of Norfolk, hereditary Earl

Marshal of England. The Great Day, indelible in the memories of those who were there
in London in 1953 or were watching on still-rather-novel television receivers at home,
began not only a summer of immense celebrations in the United Kingdom but, for the
Sovereign Lady, a life of State visits and royal tours overseas.

It was also the high noon of an opening period of near-hysteria over the glamour of
the British Crown's new phase. Euphoria and sycophancy ran riot together.
Understandably. Here was something different and intriguing – and better times to
enjoy it in. Here was a young woman on the Throne. Here was an attractive Queen and
a handsome Prince Consort, with a family of two nice small children already. A
vigorous partnership at the head of our affairs. Affection for Her Majesty was deep and
widespread; and after the Coronation – such a success, the first of the great TV
Spectaculars too – Monarchy and the Royal Family were at a peak of prestige not only
in the home country but in 'Her realms and territories beyond the seas.'

I was privileged to travel as broadcasting commentator on the epic Commonwealth
Journey, six months and 50,000 miles long, which followed the Coronation summer –
one of the earliest and certainly the longest safari of my 20 years and a-quarter-of-a-
million miles of royal tours – and one of the things impossible to forget about it was the
waves of journalistic romanticization which swept continually over the whole progress
round the globe. Interest in this new Royalty was fantastic, and mere objective reporting
far too dull for most editors. The media indulged in orgies of almost religious fervour
over what the scribes (but never the Queen) called 'a new Elizabethan Age.' The fervour
of the newspaper reports were matched by the public's appetite for it. More realistic
assessments of the travelling Royal Show came later of course; but, at first, saccharine
stories were *de rigueur*.

All the same, the attention paid to the journeys both in early and later years was a
measure of the international importance of the Queen in orbit. The tours were not only
spectacular and gave pleasure: they did good. Her Majesty and His Royal Highness
proved our best ambassadors. In country after country, their coming opened new
windows towards Britain, new aspects of other nations and other ways of life. And, after
a while, dispassionate and analytical reporting soberly disclosed the personal achievement
and lasting value of the odysseys. Later still, as world disintegration set in and narrow
insularity was all too familiar, the tours did much to keep in being the old spirit of
family-of-nations partnership.

For a long time now, the Queen has been the most widely-travelled Head of State in

The Queen and Prince Philip with legal
dignitaries in Trinidad during a tour of the
Caribbean

the world. To glance down the long list of foreign and Commonwealth tours which she
and the Duke of Edinburgh have accomplished in the last 25 years is to appreciate that
there are not many corners of the globe which they have *not* penetrated.

The tours are not picnics. Travel 'on parade' would be more the term. The frequent
and distant trips by land and air and sea – though the use of the Royal Yacht *Britannia*
often gives Her Majesty the benefit of a private residence and mobile administrative
headquarters even when far from London – involve the Queen in spells of exacting work
that are sometimes prolonged and frequently carried through in fatiguing climates.

The endless round of official engagements in the United Kingdom occupy even more
of the royal life – and these are the engagements which nowadays are the better known
and oftener pictured ones. A simple catalogue of some of the permanent fixtures is in
itself impressive: the State Openings of Parliament, the annual Official Birthday
'Trooping' ceremony, the Royal Maundy distribution of alms, solemn commemorations
in abbeys and cathedrals all over the kingdom, official services of the knightly Orders of
the Garter, the Thistle and the Bath, Remembrance Day observance, meetings of
Commonwealth ministers, receptions for learned societies, gala appearances at Covent
Garden Opera and duties at charity variety and film performances, attendances at
Guildhall banquets and City parades, visits to provincial cities and to army camps and
depots, opening docks and bridges and reservoirs and important new buildings. There
are also the appearances at agricultural shows and a whole variety of sporting events,
including of course the specially-enjoyed race meeting dates (at many of which, for many
years, the figure at Her Majesty's side was the late Duke of Norfolk, wearing then not his
Earl Marshal's but his Ascot hat).

Then there are the commitments inside the Palace: the innumerable audiences and
the Privy Council meetings, and 14 big investiture ceremonies each year. Not to forget,
either, the responsibility of acting as national host when foreign Heads of State come to
London, their visits bringing to the decorated streets those royal processional rides of
full-dress carriages and cavalry – which, apart from everything else, are a paramount
tourist attraction.

All those, and the eternal desk-work too. Every day of the year, no matter where she
may be, the Queen receives from her Government Departments and Ministers
formidable piles of dispatches, telegrams and letters. The State papers never stop: she
has much to study and sign. Twice daily the Red Boxes from the Foreign Office arrive
containing copies of reports from ambassadors, detailed minutes and messages to and

The State Opening of Parliament, which
takes place in the first week of November
every year

Introduction   19

from her representatives in her own and foreign lands. Reports of all the doings of the
House of Commons and the House of Lords land on that Palace desk too. All are read.
The Queen has a capacity for quickly scanning, rapidly absorbing – and remembering –
the essentials of what she reads, for quickly querying what is not at once clear, and for
commenting with remarkable shrewdness (and often with ringing humour) on
developments that are novel.

Though she must always be impartial, never partisan in public speech, she has
decided interests and opinions based on exceptional knowledge. Without being an
intellectual, she is crisply intelligent as well as uniquely well informed. She knows the
political and diplomatic game backwards after these years of personal experience.
One new Prime Minister – she has seen more than half a dozen come and go – emerged
from his first audience with her, and his close interrogation, with a piece of heartfelt
advice to those about to be received by the Sovereign: 'Neglect your homework at your
peril!'

The Queen herself has never been heard to complain about her work-load, but the
fact is that her duties represent a burden of responsibility from which there is at no time
a complete holiday. She 'lives over the shop' and *this* shop travels with her. She has
known from the very beginning of the reign that her 'Boxes' relentlessly invade even the
privacy of Deeside during the September interval at Balmoral. Few people in the world
can have an occupation so inescapable, homework so untransferable.

Some of the royal work may seem to be royal play. Such diversions as taking a drive
through admiring streets, dressing-up for Epsom and Ascot and Goodwood when you
are a keen racehorse owner, meeting famous figures at garden parties, going to theatres
and tournaments and Test Matches – these may appear to be little short of pure pleasure.
And in fact Her Majesty does get enjoyment from doing such things. But she cannot
relish them with the freedom of a holidaymaker because, no matter how accustomed to
the situation she may be, there is always imposed on her the tension of knowing that at
any moment, directly and probably on television too, large numbers of people are closely
regarding her. She is under unremitting examination, a specimen under a microscope,
the cynosure of all eyes.

Her Private Secretary, I remember, when he was giving his aide-mémoire to the
House of Commons Select Committee which in 1971 was considering the duties and the
costs of the Monarchy, made the point admirably: 'The strain of a long day in a
provincial town – taking a lively interest in everything, saying a kind word here and

asking a question there, always smiling and acknowledging cheers when driving in her car, sometimes for hours – has to be experienced to be properly appreciated.'

That is the strain which Her Majesty takes without question. She was well prepared for it, and it is for her an accepted part of life. And, happily, she is healthy and practised; and her professionalism is many-sided. By the time the 1950s were over and we were into the seismic 60s, she was well able to face routine and change alike and lead a very full all-round existence. Assured and in her stride, if still with a residue of shyness in her public manner, she possessed the will and strength to cope not only with official duty but also the private family preoccupations of a wife and mother, the upbringing of her children, and the directing of Palace domestic management coupled with the businesslike running of the royal dwellings and the farms and estates.

First responsibility in this field is the 600-room Buckingham Palace itself, London's best-known and possibly the world's most photographed building, its architecture the classic style of the nineteenth-century John Nash but the East Front, which unfortunately is all the public generally sees, Victorian and newly faced in 1913. This palace is the headquarters of the Monarchy and the chief 'working' royal home. But not the only one. Windsor Castle, an equally powerful magnet to tourists with its towers and battlements and lovely St George's Chapel, spiritual home of the Order of the Garter, is almost as much lived-in and worked-in at certain times as Buckingham Palace is. It is certainly a favourite residence of the Queen and her family. The castle rears itself nobly and massively above the River Thames, 20 miles west of London, on a mound where William the Conqueror built a fort nine centuries ago.

Those other metropolitan landmarks, St James's Palace and Kensington Palace and Hampton Court – they are Crown property too. The Houses of Parliament are Her Majesty's 'Palace of Westminster', and the Tower of London is a royal fortress whose Yeomen Warders wear the Queen's cipher on their Tudor uniforms.

The fine old Palace of Holyroodhouse in Edinburgh is the royal home and headquarters in the Northern Realm, Scotland. When the Sovereign is in residence there – usually for a week in summer – she is ceremonially attended by a picturesque company of bowmen who are the Queen's Body Guard for Scotland, the Royal Company of Archers. They guard the Queen when she is in the Scottish capital just as the historic and even more eye-catching Gentlemen at Arms and the Yeomen of the Guard do when she is in England. (The Yeomen, incidentally, are a proud and distinct corps, all ex-soldiers and of impeccable record. They are not to be confused with that other impressive body, the Tower's Yeomen Warders – and must never be called 'Beefeaters!')

In addition to the State palaces, the Queen has houses which she owns personally and privately. First, Balmoral Castle in Aberdeenshire, her residence in Scotland, a baronial pile of granite pepper-pot towers which was constructed by Prince Albert in the middle of the last century and dearly loved by Queen Victoria when she had become obsessed with the Highlands. Balmoral is a joy to Victoria's great-great-granddaughter too. For it is to this remote house, set among the hills of Deeside, that she and her family gratefully repair for a few weeks of late summer and autumn leave from the limelight. For many years, however, it has been their custom to make one public appearance in Scotland during the vacation, to visit and enjoy the most famous of annual Highland Gatherings at nearby Braemar.

The other well-known private property is Sandringham, the big house in northern East Anglia, set in a rich open countryside near King's Lynn. Sandringham was built by Edward the Seventh when he was Prince of Wales. A country retreat for generations of the Royal Family, it has recently undergone demolition and restoration work; and at the Queen's wish parts of the house and estate have been prepared so as to be accessible to the public. But Sandringham remains a royal home, with many special memories, a place of history both happy and sad, very personally associated with the Royal House of Windsor and today with the Queen's own family.

When we talk of the Royal *Family* it is not merely a convenient phrase. 'The Royals' *are* a distinct and close-knit family, much in each other's company, not only sharing many personal interests and off-duty activities but co-operating and engagingly assisting in the official duties of the Monarchy. With this family, Her Majesty can share the load.

In her husband, the extrovert Prince Philip, Duke of Edinburgh, who in age is five years her senior, the Queen has a quick-minded and indefatigable partner, a man with interests and activities enough for half-a-dozen average human beings, a remarkable helpmeet to monarch and monarchy. They make a good team, the Queen and he – and not altogether by reason of matching qualities but rather, it has always seemed to me, because they are excellently complementary in character. Certainly, with the robust and restless Prince Philip on hand, a good public speaker, a natural sociologist, a modern sportsman and aviator, a student of technology, an impatient innovator suffering no outmoded ways gladly, the British Monarchy could scarcely be dull or display only a placid ceremonial image.

Prince Philip has a talent for public life – a talent rivalled only perhaps by the similar

The Royal Family make friends with
some of the calves on the Balmoral Castle
estate

Introduction   23

aptitude of his mother-in-law, that shining national institution, Her Majesty Queen
Elizabeth the Queen Mother. As old as the century but sparklingly perennial, she still
delights in having a diary crammed with engagements and holds an enormous number of
official positions, including the Chancellorship of the University of London, whose
duties she tackles joyfully and without stint. She photographs well, knows it and likes it.
For years she has been Fleet Street cameramen's 'pin-up' because she tries to see that
they get the pictures they want. The news photographers are not the most popular boys
in the form on royal occasions. In the view of over-anxious organizers at least, they tend
to get in the way. But the Queen Mother remembers that, like herself, they have a job
of work to do. Once I saw a fussy official trying to push an accredited cameraman out of
her path. Her Majesty noticed the incident and said with a smile: 'Please don't do that.
Mr So-and-so and I are old friends.'

She is to many minds, not only pressmen's, Royalty's 'top of the pops'; and is widely
known, with genuine affection, simply as 'The Queen Mum'.

Then there are her six grandchildren. Of the four children of the Queen and Prince
Philip, the elder two are now grown-up and living busy lives of their own. Prince Charles,
Heir to the Throne, born a year after his parents' marriage and splendidly invested as
Prince of Wales at Caernarvon Castle twenty years later, gained a good degree at Trinity
College, Cambridge, and became an R.A.F. pilot before joining the Royal Navy in 1971.
In so doing he was following his father's footsteps and the career tradition of his
mother's family. When ashore he has managed to carry out royal as well as naval duties;
and inevitably a world of public engagements lies ahead of him. That he will do them
well is certain, for he is a popular success already and has his father's natural capacity for
bringing an easy but inquiring informality into every kind of encounter.

Princess Anne, two years younger than Charles, who has become known as a world-
class horsewoman, married a fellow rider, Captain Mark Phillips of the Queen's
Dragoon Guards, when she was 23. Like her mother's marriage celebrations 26 years
before, her wedding in the Abbey in 1973 came to the public as a *bonne-bouche* of
romance and a radiant gleam of happiness in a time of national economic gloom.

Young Prince Andrew and Prince Edward, born in 1960 and 1964, more than a decade
after Charles and Anne, have been brought up out of the public eye. Lively and
personable schoolboys, they are still far from ceremonial duties and the glare which
surrounds them.

In the wider circle of the Royal Family there are others of the Queen's relations –

Leaving No. 10 Downing Street after
dining with Sir Winston Churchill before
his retirement from office

besides her sister, Princess Margaret – who, adult and active, are notably felicitous in performance of official tasks and who increasingly take weight off the shoulders of the Monarch, enlivening the public scene as they do so. The much liked Princess Alexandra of Kent is one of these, a first cousin of the Queen but ten years younger. She has the gusto of her own generation and the grace of her late mother, Princess Marina. Next, her lively Yorkshire sister-in-law, the Duchess of Kent, formerly Miss Katharine Worsley. Her husband, the soldier Duke of Kent too. Also, seen more and more, the Duke of Gloucester and his young Danish-born Duchess. They are all active in what Prince Philip, with characteristic candour, has called 'the Firm.'

And the firm, whose business is royalty, has been flexibly at the centre of many changes which have swept through the realm in the last quarter of a century. Not only has the British Empire vanished – its dissolution began in George the Sixth's later days and afterwards quickened to completion – but the pattern of the 'free association' of States called the Commonwealth has altered and diminished too, territory after territory achieving independence, often of a republican nature, though acknowledging the Queen as link and leader-titular. (The Queen has publicly described the change from Empire to Commonwealth as a 'beneficial and civilised metamorphosis'.) Britain itself has shrunk and is no longer a major World Power. Membership of the European Community has raised questions about our national Sovereignty itself. Inflation and its economic doldrums – self-doubt too – have struck painfully at the old motherland; and the British Isles have come sadly to experience at first hand the murderous terrorism which in earlier years we had comprehended only as a contagion rife in foreign countries. We live in years of both wonder and wickedness. In recording them, the history books will set down the marvels of space travel and moon landings together with the miseries of Suez and Cyprus and Ulster.

It was with the experience of many cataclysmic events already, then, that the Queen and Prince Philip came to the celebration of their Silver Wedding on 20 November 1972 – a year which for the British people was as perplexed and anxious as the year of the royal marriage itself, in 1947, when an impoverished and rationed nation was wearily counting the cost of war. But, rightly, Silver Wedding day was no unsmiling occasion but a bright moment of personal and national thanksgiving, seized by the public as a spectacle briefly relieving the encompassing melancholy. The Queen marked the anniversary by taking a stroll through City crowds after a Guildhall lunch and an Abbey service to which she and her husband had invited 100 couples who had been married on the same day.

Anyone who was in Guildhall that Silver Wedding afternoon for the lunch will remember the sight and sound of a Queen more smilingly relaxed than on any public occasion of her life. When she rose to address the company she immediately teased herself over what through the years had become a widely-mimicked cliché in most of her set speeches. She said: 'I think everybody really will concede that on this day of all days I *should* begin my speech with the words "My husband and I!"' The speech from its start to finish set the audience applauding, but more particularly it set them into surprised laughter. For this was a figure they had not known before. She cracked jokes and made gestures. She remembered the Bishop who, when asked his opinion of sin, replied that he was against it; and she went on: 'If I'm asked what I think of family life after 25 years of marriage, I can answer with equal simplicity: I am for it.'

This seemed for many people a glimpse of the real Queen, not the lady they had so often seen in public as a serious and reserved person, evidently not enjoying the publicity, her natural verve overlaid no doubt by that conscientiousness and awareness of responsibility which have made her public appearances less telling than television-conditioned onlookers expect. And it was indeed a glimpse of the very feminine person her family and close friends know when the photographers and the crowds are not present, a lady with her spontaneous sense of fun unleashed, her conversation full of effervescence, awelessness – and tolerance. (If only over-anxious Royal Visit arrangers in the towns, worried stiff over details and misguidedly fearing royal censure when some little *contretemps* occurs, could see how the Visitor laughs when she gets home!)

Not that there is any double standard about her. She does not wear a false mask in public and is someone quite different behind it. Only in the sense that she prefers being private to being a floodlit centre of attention can it be said that there are two Elizabeths, for her home life and her ceremonial life have the same honesty. The official tour and the outing with the corgis both show the true person. This is a lady who is nothing if not genuine, for whom 'putting on an act' is not so much foreign to her as utterly impossible. More photographed than a film star, she never behaves like one. Sometimes young television producers wish that she *would*. But though the Christmas Day broadcasts have in the main been stiffer than hoped for, they are sincere – and they are *her*.

Never for this Queen the mistake her uncle made in his months of sad failure as a king: Edward the Eighth believed that he could have a life of self-indulgence behind the scenes and yet present himself for respect as Guardian of the Nation on stage. His niece's private and public ways do not clash and are both unblemished.

Yet she is sensible and modern and adaptable as a public person and as a parent too. She has abolished such archaic snob-shows as debutantes' Presentation Courts and has made her garden parties mammoth gatherings at which the viscounts and viceroys are lost in a sea of worthy village postmistresses and votive priests of trade unions. She has fundamentally altered the way of educating the royal young, and, in contrast to the old style of teaching princes by having them tutored in palace seclusion, her children have from an early age gone away to school like other boys and girls – and, once there, been treated like the others too.

As much informality and as little fuss as possible, but preserving traditional ceremonies and loved customs – that is the life-style of the Royal Family. Meeting as many people as possible, and from as many walks of life as possible, hoping that they will be people with natural good manners but no phoney kowtowing – that is a predilection of the Queen. Her habit of going about and mixing freely is something she has deliberately not diminished in spite of mounting public anxiety and increased, though unobtrusive police precautions – which were urgently stepped-up in 1974 after the alarming incident in the Mall when an armed man, shooting passers-by and narrowly missing the young couple who were his target, easily held up a royal car a few yards from Buckingham Palace and tried to kidnap Princess Anne as she and her husband rode back from an official engagement.

The protecting of V.I.P.s, especially the Royal Family, is a heavy problem. The Queen knows the risks but will not countenance being cut off from her people. If she goes on an outside engagement, then she goes announced and free to move, not to be hustled in and out of armour-plated cars by trigger-happy G-men along routes cleared of spectators.

Travelling often with Her Majesty and the others has taught me that their work is risky though guarded by goodwill, and that they carry out the work with the risks faced unhesitatingly. They do their duties and—it is but factual reporting to say this – do them with courage as well as amiability and efficiency. The Queen was cool and calm, dodging not one minute of ordained programmes, when riding through tense Accra with a frightened Nkrumah and when facing hostile separatists in the city of Quebec. Not only level-headed and brave: graceful and gleaming too, even then. The régime has radiance.

Our 'Second Elizabethan Age' has great and benign achievements. With her life now over the half-century mark and her reign occupying half that span, the Queen can contemplate a Britain which to use the trendy term, has 'kept its cool', has eschewed conquest and oppression, has liberated colonial millions and (controversial though this is)

has made our country a haven for other breeds whom nationalism has rendered homeless. And *our* thinkers and adventurers, this era's men of lunar exploration and nuclear discovery, make the Tudor giants look Lilliputian.

Economically and spiritually ailing though we have been, the central institution, the Monarchy, is healthy, a prize to hold on to as times get better. The royal Windsors have at least inherited from the House of Hanover a stability which the Tudors and Stuarts by no means possessed. And Elizabeth of Windsor steadily presides over a Commonwealth which, however slimmed and loosened its ties, is still the only major association of states which links countries of the developed and under-developed worlds.

But to return to the story-in-pictures which this book tells. The present royal era, critics say, is the era of the image makers and an adman's dream: if the Monarchy is hallowed, it is hallowed by camera. Well, no harm in that; and the photographs speak well for themselves and their subjects. Royalty must not only work but be seen at work; and enjoyment of what it all looks like is perfectly proper. The Queen and her family are not something secret. They are not held in mindless awe, nor indeed exempt from cool scrutiny, plebiscite and debate, periodical censure. No harm in that either. The important thing is that the Monarchy remains a puissant force, Britain's most agreeably visible element of continuity. It gives dignity to days of triviality.

The Royal Family are able to represent and bring recognition to something of the best in the national life. We can be grateful for the wholesome presence of the leader of the Family, Her Majesty the Queen, trusted heir to a thousand years of kingship, a symbol yet not an abstraction, our emblem of tradition and instrument of change.

Prince Charles receiving the Freedom
of the City of London

On the way to the Trooping the Colour
ceremony: Prince Charles, the Queen
Mother, Lady Sarah Armstrong-Jones
and Princess Anne

Prince Charles in the Navy: aboard
H.M.S. *Jupiter*

Prince Charles giving his oath to the
Queen on his Investiture as Prince of
Wales at Caernarvon Castle

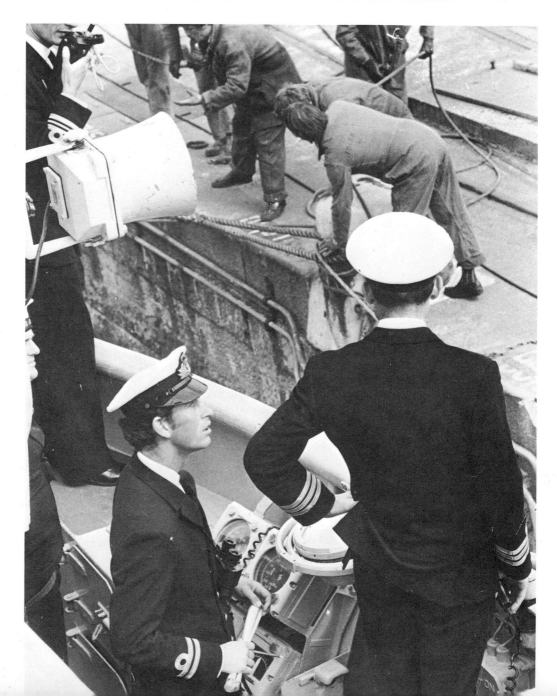

Prince Philip sailing *Coweslip* in one of the Royal Regatta Races at Cowes

Inspection of the Royal Company of Archers, the ceremonial guard of the monarch when at Holyroodhouse

Princess Anne and Captain Mark Phillips
at Amberley Horse Show

The wedding of Princess Anne and
Captain Mark Phillips at Westminster
Abbey

At Windsor Castle, Christmas 1971.
Standing, left to right, Earl of Snowdon,
Duke of Kent, Prince Michael of Kent,
Prince Philip, Earl of St Andrews, Prince
Charles, Prince Andrew, Angus Ogilvy,
James Ogilvy. *Seated,* Princess Margaret,
Duchess of Kent holding Lord Nicholas
Windsor, The Queen Mother, the Queen,
Princess Anne, Marina Ogilvy, Princess
Alexandra. *In front,* Lady Sarah
Armstrong-Jones, Viscount Linley,
Prince Edward, Lady Helen Windsor.

The Queen and Prince Philip on the
occasion of their Silver Wedding

The Queen attends Evensong at the Chapel
Royal of St Peter-ad-Vincula in the Tower
of London, escorted by the Yeomen
Warders